THIS BOOK I

. . . .

THE MOST UGLY/BIG-HEADED/
PROVOCATIVE / SILLY/DIVINE/
EROTIC PISCES LOVER I KNOW.
FROM

. . . .

P.S. TAKE A GOOD LOOK AT PAGE(S)

. . . .

PISCES

A CORGI BOOK 0 552 12837 6

First publication in Great Britain
PRINTING HISTORY
Corgi edition published 1986

Corgi Books are published by Transworld Publishers Ltd.,
61-63 Uxbridge Road, Ealing, London W5 5SA, in Australia by
Transworld Publishers (Australia) Pty. Ltd., 15-23 Helles Avenue,
Moorebank, NSW 2170, and in New Zealand by Transworld
Publishers (N.Z.) Ltd., Cnr. Moselle and Waipareira Avenues,
Henderson, Auckland.

Made and printed in Great Britain by the
Guernsey Press Co. Ltd., Guernsey, Channel Islands.

Ian Heath's
LOVE SIGNS
PISCES

CORGI BOOKS

PISCES

FEBRUARY 19 - MARCH 20

TWELFTH SIGN OF THE ZODIAC
SYMBOL : THE FISHES
RULING PLANETS : JUPITER, NEPTUNE
NUMBER : SEVEN
COLOURS : SEA-GREEN, VIOLET
FLOWER : GARDENIA
DAY : THURSDAY
GEMS : OPAL, AQUAMARINE
METAL : PLATINUM

The PISCEAN lover is.....

. . . . .A DREAMER . . . .

. . . . . . EASILY INFLUENCED. . . . . . .

. . . . . . UNUSUALLY CREATIVE . . . . .

. . . . WAYWARD . . . .

. . . . A NON-STOP TALKER . . . . .

. . . . A GOOD HOUSE-KEEPER. . . .

. . . . . . VERY RESPONSIVE . . . . . .

. . . . AND ALWAYS SMILING.

The **PISCES** likes to make love..

. . . . . UNDER A PALM-TREE. . . . . . .

. . . . .ON A SNOOKER-TABLE. . . . . .

. . . . . IN A RAILWAY CARRIAGE . . . .

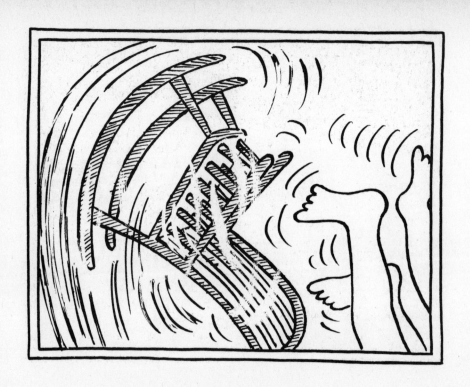

. . . . .IN A ROCKING-CHAIR. . . . .

. . . . . IN FRONT OF THE TELLY . . . . .

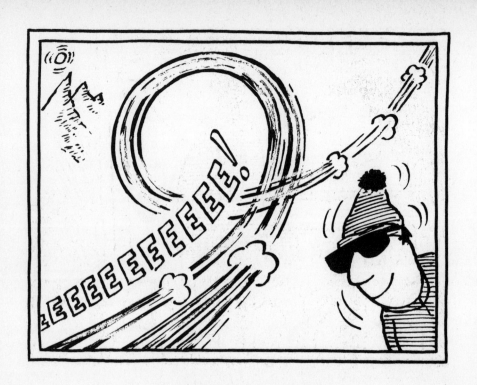

. . . . AND ON SKIS .

The PISCEAN lover's bedroom..

. . . . . .IS FULL OF BOOKS. . . . . . .

. . . . . .HAS LOTS OF PILLOWS. . . . . .

. . . . . . AND A BATH.

MMMMMMMM

To turn on
a male
PISCES......

. . . . . . BLOW UP HIS NOSE. . . . .

. . . . . . RUFFLE HIS HAIR . . . . . .

. . AND WHISPER SWEET NOTHINGS.

MMMMMMMM

To turn on a female PISCES.....

. . . . . .BRUSH HER HAIR. . . . . .

. . . . WEAR COWBOY BOOTS . . . . .

. . . AND GIVE HER A MASSAGE.

. . . . . . .THE EYEBROWS. . . . .

. . . . . .SOLES OF THE FEET. . . . . .

. . . . . .THE LEFT ELBOW. . . . . .

. . . . . AND THE CHEEKS.

APHRODISIACS
♡ FOR THE ♡
PISCEAN
LOVER

SPAGHETTI

HONEY CHEESECAKE

BANANA AND TUNA
SANDWICHES

MANGO MILKSHAKE

SQUID

The PISCEAN lover likes to receive....

. . . . . A CRYSTAL VASE . . . . . .

. . . . **FLOWERS** . . . .

. . . . . . AND TOYS.

PISCES AND LOVERS
HEART RATINGS

♡♡♡♡♡ POW!! ZAP!!

♡♡♡♡ MAGIC~BUT NOT 'IT'

♡♡♡ FUN! FUN! FUN!

♡♡ PRETTY AWFUL

♡ GRIM~RUN FAST!

PISCES and...

...ARIES

EXCITEMENT IN ALL AREAS OF THIS
PARTNERSHIP COULD MEAN
SOMETHING GOOD.

♡ ♡ ♡ ♡

...TAURUS

EXCELLENT PROSPECTS
FOR AN ARDENT ATTACHMENT.
ENJOY IT!

♡ ♡ ♡ ♡

PISCES and...

...GEMINI

AN UNHAPPY PAIRING.
-BOTH WILL BECOME BORED.
FORGET IT!

♡ ♡

...CANCER

FLASH! BANG! WALLOP!
COMPATIBLE IN EVERY WAY.

♡ ♡ ♡ ♡ ♡

o o o o o o o o o o o o o o o o o o o

PISCES and

...LEO
AN IMPOSSIBLE MATCH.
FORGET IT!

♡

...VIRGO
A BORING AND SHORT-LIVED AFFAIR.

♡ ♡

...LIBRA
NO! NO! NO!

♡

PISCES and...

...SCORPIO

SOOPER-DOOPER!!!

♡ ♡ ♡ ♡ ♡

...SAGITTARIUS

GREAT FUN FOR A WHILE.

♡ ♡ ♡

...CAPRICORN

THIS STARTS OFF WITH A BANG,
AND MAY NOT FIZZLE OUT.

♡ ♡ ♡ ♡

PISCES and

...AQUARIUS

GREAT FROLICKINGS,
FUN AND FIREWORKS!
COULD LAST.

♡ ♡ ♡ ♡

...PISCES

MANY MAGICAL MOMENTS
DURING THIS BRIEF LIASON.

♡ ♡ ♡

o o o o o o o o o o o o o o o o o o o o

Annoying **PISCEAN** habits are...

. . . . . EATING IN BED . . . . . .

. . . . CONSTANTLY SLEEPING . . . .

. . . . AND RARELY WASHING.

FAMOUS PISCEAN LOVERS

'BUFFALO BILL' CODY
RUDOLPH NUREYEV · CHOPIN
ELIZABETH TAYLOR · JERRY LEWIS
LIZA MINELLI · AUGUSTE RENOIR
JILLY COOPER · ALBERT EINSTEIN

SIDNEY POITIER · NIJINSKY
EDWARD KENNEDY · DAVID NIVEN
MICHELANGELO · VICTOR HUGO
PETER FONDA · URSULA ANDRESS
KENNETH WILLIAMS · PAM AYRES
JASPER CARROT · JEAN HARLOW
GEORGE HARRISON · MAX WALL
JOHNNY CASH · CYD CHARISSE
GLENN MILLER · LYN REDGRAVE
HANDEL · FATS DOMINO

To keep your

PISCEAN

lover. . . . . . .

. . . . . DARN HIS/HER SOCKS. . . . . .

. . . . . NEVER DISAGREE . . . . . .

. . . . . . BE ROMANTIC.

To get rid of your **PISCEAN** lover........

. . . . . KILL HIS/HER PLANTS. . . . .

. . . .INSULT HIS/HER FRIENDS. . . .

. . . . . KICK HIS/HER CAT.